Genius comes in strange packages.
I knew that the Punkmeister had it the first time I heard the immortal couplet:

"1969 OK
All across the USA"

**THIS ONE'S FOR NATHALIE**
**LONG MAY HER POWER ROAR**

Copyright © 2005 Mick Rock

This edition © 2005 Omnibus Press
(A division of Music Sales Limited)

Designed by Adrian Cross

ISBN: 1.84449.526.4
Order No: OP50479

**Exclusive Distributors**
Music Sales Limited,
8/9 Frith Street,
London W1D 3JB, UK.

Music Sales Corporation,
257 Park Avenue South,
New York, NY 10010, USA.

Macmillan Distribution Services,
53 Park West Drive,
Derrimut, Vic 3030,
Australia.

**To the Music Trade only:**
Music Sales Limited,
8/9 Frith Street,
London W1D 3JB, UK.

Printed and bound in Singapore.

A catalogue record for this book is available
from the British Library.

Visit Omnibus Press on the web at
www.omnibuspress.com

# RAW POWER

# INTRODUCTION

I was in the middle of my daily ten minute headstand when the phone rang. Mostly I ignore the calls under those circumstances, but this day I sensed that I should take the call. It was the excited voice of my favorite photo assistant, Cody. "The Stooges are back in the studio with Iggy," he blurted. "All of them?" I queried. "The brothers. Not James Williamson," he replied. This was indeed news, for the Asheton Brothers are with Iggy, the core Stooges - starting with the original 1967 lineup with Dave Alexander. It was as if the Younger brothers, Cole and Bob, had hooked up with Jesse James again. Well, not quite. The James Gang only robbed banks. The Stooges were in the business of pillaging psyches.

My young friend hadn't even been born the last time this mutant bunch had worked their menacing mojo. Was this really that important to him? "Oh yes," he shot back, "This is the motherf__ing Stooges. They were punk before punk was punk." Now that, I thought, is a fact.

It transpired that Scott and Ron were working on four tracks for Iggy's latest solo album. Once the word hit the streets, the demand swiftly grew for The Stooges to tread the boards again. Not only their original fans, but also young rock 'n roll fans of new bands like The Strokes, The Kills, Razorlight, etc., wanted to taste them live. For The Stooges, they understood, were the absolute original purveyors of what David Bowie once described as "nihilistic rock, which totally fascinated me… I love nihilism…" Raw, rampant, deliberately, definitely, insanely primal - that was The Stooges in their heyday.

So it's back to the future, methought. More evidence that things do indeed move in cycles… My next thought was that the time had come to buy back the rights to my original *Raw Power* book and remix (i.e., redesign) it to more appropriately reflect these unique artists and our legendary photo sessions. The original book was the first of a series of collections of photos which I have published in recent years and I had not been smart enough to secure and control the quality of the design and production. It was admired by the hardcore Stooges fan, because it did at least give them access to the photos, but it didn't present the images to their best advantage. This time I would get it right.

I also wanted to have Jim Osterberg's overt stamp of approval. For the first version, he had given me a succinct one-liner: "Mick Rock is one crazy photographer," but for this new improved tome, it was mandatory that he write a full-blooded foreword. This is an artist I have known for many years, and for whom I maintain a deep and abiding respect. I needed him to love the way I present his image, so I worked to bring him on board. For these photos, as the passage of time has borne out, are the ones that defined him forever to his public. When most people think of Iggy Pop they see the *Raw Power* cover in their minds' eye. That's just the way it worked out.

The first version of the book garnered a certain amount of press, especially in the UK, which has spewed out an army of hip and articulate young rock critics since the early Seventies. And they all love Iggy (and the long-dormant Stooges). He provides a great persona to hang an encyclopaedia of colorful adjectives on… The *NME*, in discussing the virtues of the original book, dubbed me "The Dennis Hopper of Rock Photography". I wasn't sure if the writer had in mind the specific image of Mr. Hopper's role as the rampant, semi-demented shutterbug in *Apocalypse Now* or was referring to his anarchic, chaotic, freewheeling lifestyle of the late Sixties and Seventies, which forever framed him. It should also be noted that Dennis is actually a very excellent stills man in his own right.

At the time I remember telling a friend that if I had to be compared to an actor, I would rather be thought of as the Laurence Olivier of Rock Photography. But, given the facts on the ground, maybe *NME* had it right.

In a recent interview, Jim gave insight into what initially propelled his art and the formation of The Stooges: "It occurred to me that the general idea of music could be an escape from the drabness I saw around me growing up... that I could make white, suburban, delinquent music... that I could make a new musical form. And that to do that it was necessary to work with people who knew even less than I did. So I enlisted Ron and Scott and Co."

He also discussed Stooges Mark II, with new guitarist and co-songwriter James Williamson (Ron was relegated to bass), "who could actually play 'Johnny B Goode' which the rest of us definitely couldn't." James was technically more accomplished than the others and this new synthesis, as Jim stated, produced "a music that was more musically complicated and lyrically provocative." The result of this was, of course, *Raw Power*, which stands as the most potent studio expression of the nihilism and anarchy embodied by The Stooges.

There is a school of serious aficionados who would argue that this was rock music's most explosive and dangerous moment; that the punk that came along in the mid and late Seventies was a pale reflection of the foaming, foraging Stooges in their prime. This is the stuff of myth and legend: The Stooges as rock 'n roll exorcists, as progenitors of a new, anarchic order. Heady stuff, as it turns out.

Iggy now articulates more fully on the sources of inspiration for his uninhibited and groundbreaking live performances: "I don't analyze

it too much. Like Elvis said 'I can't help myself.' It comes from the nature of amplified music. It wasn't there before things were plugged in. Some of it maybe comes from deep childhood problems – anger, fear, etc. Probably lots of fear..." he laughs. Or as Scott more succinctly puts it, "Jim had a need to be with his audience."

As often in those early days, I was lucky with my obsessions. I had the right instincts for the times, and I seized images that still resonate. You can't plan stuff like that. Part of the appeal of The Stooges was that they had clearly tapped into something totally unique, something that had not been expressed before. Their music and performance was so 'up yours', so raw, so 'in your face', that most audiences didn't know how to handle it. And so that steamy Friday night in July 1972 at La Scala Theatre, King's Cross, I witnessed a frontal assault led by a personality who was already in my mind more mythological than human. His appeal was omnisexual: he was physically very beautiful; the silver hair and silver trousers only added to the sense of the mythological. He seemed to have emerged from some bizarre, primal hinterland, so much bigger than life, emoting and projecting a tingling menace. From a modern perspective, it's clear that he was by any standards a cultural revolutionary, operating well ahead of his time.

The cover for the album was lensed that night. The album was not yet recorded and it would be several months before it was finally released in the spring of 1973. Iggy was never consulted about the cover or the layout. That was organized between his manager Tony Defries and CBS. I was only a pawn in their game, and had assumed they would run it by Jim before going to print. But they didn't. As he says in the liner notes to the new mix of the album he produced in 1997: "The cover was dictated to me... I hated it. I thought they were taking the piss with the monster lettering and everything.

Since then I realize that… they did me a favor. The photograph is beautiful, the lettering is memorable, and nobody would've had the guts. I wouldn't have… to put that cover out like that. So they did me a solid."

The truth, as I came to understand it, was that the record deal with CBS Records only came about because of the vision and passion of David Bowie. Defries took Iggy on because David bugged him. He didn't even want the rest of the group. He wasn't interested in bands per se. He wanted to 'groom stars' (his words). The Stooges were in the wilderness. They couldn't sell records, they had serious drug habits, they couldn't even get a gig in the US anymore. Their reputation for chaos and mayhem preceded them wherever they went. They were a nightmare to manage and weren't going to put any serious money into anyone's pocket, including their own. Who needed it?

But the Bowie connection worked serious magic at that key moment and *Raw Power* was nursed into being. David's star had risen so fast in the summer/autumn of 1972, that he no longer had time to repeat the production genius he had exhibited on Mott The Hoople's 'All The Young Dudes' and Lou Reed's *Transformer*, even if Iggy had wanted him to. And when *Raw Power* originally came out there was no production credit. It was spawned rather than produced in the traditional sense. Iggy and his gang just want into the studio and banged and wailed away in frenzied desperation, and later Bowie, at the request of the record company, went in on a rescue mission and mixed all the crazy elements into a form that they found acceptable.

In 1997 Jim took the tapes and did an entire new mix on his own

And on the cover of the remixed version he finally gets his long-deserved producer's credit. To my mind, both the original 1972 and the 1997 remix stand up aesthetically in their own quite different right. Which one I play depends on what mood I'm in. Both are true to the source material and the spirit in which it was rendered.

Jim recently reminisced on the mania and terminal chaos of that period: "There was mess piled upon mess waiting for the release of that record." No-one knew how to handle it or the band. The music didn't fit into any recognizable category and the Stooges were speaking in tongues. "I became very unsound. I was on a mission basically to destroy the world. By the time the record came out management and the record company had basically washed their hands of us. I had a band and it had gone to hell."

There was no promotion for the album, no live performances or TV appearances to spread the word. Their goose was cooked and no-one wanted to partake of it. According to Defries it took over 20 years to recoup the advances and production costs. The Stooges had nowhere to go. Success wasn't part of their vocabulary. It was so over, it was funereal. As Iggy says, his band had gone to hell… phew.

But it's now over 30 years later and on their 2004 reunion tour they played 40 venues in 15 countries and their audiences were ecstatic. Although severely weathered, Iggy, Scott and Ron (on guitar again with a new bass player) have skewered the passage of time (and they still sport plenty of hair and dark enthusiasm). Their performance as headliners at Little Steven's Garage Festival on Randall's Island, New York in August 2004 proved why their legend is still so strong. Iggy invited everyone who could fit up on stage for

COPYRIGHT © BOB GRUEN

'No Fun' and The Stooges tore it up. One enthusiastic writer extolled their performance as 'something akin to that old time religion'.

The Stooges have found their once and future audience. So sometimes there is a kind of justice. As my friend Wayne Kramer (guitarist of The MC5) puts it: "Sometimes you achieve iconic status by being the last man standing." He should know… another Detroit survivor of drugs, insanity and mayhem. It's a hard life for artists operating so many years ahead of their time. It doesn't pay the bills, and any respect garnered is of the meager variety. The very unlikely art of the very unlikely Stooges has finally felt the warm embrace of a modern audience. It's been a slow train getting to this point, but at least they're still around to enjoy it. Jim, Ron, and Scott (and James), this book is my homage to the glory and genius that was and is you…

Gimme danger indeed…

**Mick Rock**
New York City, January 2005

010

"Sometimes the jagged art of the abandoned and the wasted emerges fully formed from the slime and stench of the gutter."

Stefan George, 1863

012

HERE WAS A 'MONSTER' IN THE SHAKESPEARIAN SENSE, ELEMENTAL, A FORCE OF NATURE. HE WAS LIKE SOMETHING CAGED AND VERY ANGRY ABOUT IT. SOMETHING DREAMED UP BY KARL JUNG...DIONYSIUS IN SILVER, BREAKING OUT...

**FOREWORD** SOMEHOW, I LANDED IN ENGLAND ON A BA JET. IT WAS 1972, I THINK. JAMES WAS WITH ME. WE WERE IMMEDIATELY DETAINED; ON SUSPICION OF VAGRANCY, THEY SAID. THEY BUILT A LITTLE CELL FOR US IN HEATHROW OUT OF MOVABLE WALLS. TONY D. CAME HOURS LATER AND SPRUNG US. WE WERE CARRYING THE SEEDS OF OUR VERY NEW AND DIFFERENT MUSIC. IT WAS TRUE ROCKING. MOST MUSIC WAS SHIT. JAMES WAS A CRACKPOT. I WAS OUT OF MY MIND.

WE TRIED TO STAY AT THE PORTOBELLO HOTEL FOR A WHILE, BUT WE COULDN'T WORK THE SHOWERS, AND I DIDN'T LIKE THE ENGLISH HIPPIES AND THE CRAMPED QUARTERS. I DIDN'T MUCH LIKE JAMES EITHER, BUT HE WAS CARRYING SOME OF THE SEEDS.

WE MOVED TO THE ROYAL GARDENS, ON KENSINGTON PARK. THIS WAS BETTER. IT WAS A BRIDAL SUITE, BECAUSE THEY THOUGHT IGGY WAS A GIRL'S NAME. WE HAD TO SLEEP TOGETHER ON THE FIRST NIGHT, 'TIL I FOUND THE MURPHY BED. I BOUGHT A CHEETAH JACKET AT KEN MARKET, AND WALKED AROUND THE PARK A LOT, TRYING TO THINK. 'SEARCH & DESTROY' CAME FROM THE PARK; 'I'M SICK OF YOU' CAME FROM THE MURPHY BED. I HAD A HUGE BATHTUB THERE WITH A TEMPERATURE CONTROL, AND SOMETIMES I'D GO DOWNSTAIRS AND HAVE MY HAIR DONE. I HAD LUNCH THERE ONCE WITH DAVID BOWIE. HE ATE SUGAR CUBES, AND I ATE HONEY.

A MAN NAMED LAURENCE MYERS GAVE US HIS HOUSE IN ST. JOHN'S WOOD. I LIKED TO WALK AROUND THE CRICKET PITCH. 'I GOTTA RIGHT' CAME ALONG ABOUT THEN. LAURENCE WAS AN ASSOCIATE OF TONY D., AND HE RAN A COMPANY CALLED GEM MUSIC, A SONGWRITING MILL WITH A BIG IMPRESSIVE FRONT OFFICE FOR THE BOSS, AND A SMALL HALLWAY OFF ONE SIDE WITH FIVE OR SIX TINY WORKROOMS FOR THE WRITERS, EACH WITH AN UPRIGHT PIANO.

THEY TOLD ME 'BUILD ME UP, BUTTERCUP' WAS WRITTEN THERE. I GUESS THAT'S COOL. ANYWAY, JAMES SPILLED HIS CORNFLAKES AND MILK ON THE GUY'S CARPET ONE MORNING AND NEVER REALLY GOT AROUND TO CLEANING IT UP, SO WE KIND OF HAD TO MOVE ON, AND ENDED UP IN THE (STOOGE) HOUSE ON SEYMOUR WALK, WHERE I MET MICK ROCK.

SEYMOUR WALK WAS A FAIRLY RITZY LITTLE STREET OFF THE FULHAM ROAD, AND THIS IS WHERE THE STOOGES REGROUPED AND ULTIMATELY CREATED THE *RAW POWER* ALBUM. THIS WAS AN INTENSELY CREATIVE PERIOD IN MY LIFE. THREE IMPORTANT THINGS HAPPENED ONCE THE ASHETONS - RON & SCOTT, JOINED US IN BRITAIN: 1. REGULAR BAND REHEARSALS. 2. A SINGLE GIG, AND 3. RECORDING *RAW POWER*.

MICK'S PHOTOS (BASICALLY) SHOW US AT WORK, AND WE LOVED OUR WORK, AND WERE VERY CONFIDENT OF ITS QUALITY, AND IT SHOWS.

OUR PRACTICE ROOM WAS A HOLE IN THE GROUND. THE MUSIC WAS KIND OF VIOLENT; WHEN WE PLAYED OUR GIG I REMEMBER I KEPT FALLING DOWN BECAUSE THE SONGS WERE SO FAST AND THERE WERE SO MANY LOUD WORDS TO BE SAID.

THE SONG TITLES WERE THINGS LIKE 'GIMME SOME SKIN', 'I'M SICK OF YOU', 'FRESH RAG', 'PRIVATE PARTS', 'SCENE OF THE CRIME', 'I GOTTA RIGHT'…AND WE PRACTICED 'EM OVER AND OVER DOWN IN THE HOLE. WE RECORDED SOME OF THESE AT THE TIME IN SHORT STUDIO SESSIONS, JUST TO SEE. NO ONE ENCOURAGED US IN THIS, REALLY, BECAUSE THE STUFF SOUNDED LIKE… THE OPPOSITE OF MONEY. SO WE WROTE SOME MORE, A LITTLE MORE FORMAL, AND THOSE BECAME *RAW POWER*.

LIFE AS LIVED AT SEYMOUR WALK WAS KIND OF A WEIRD FLOATING PERMANENT VACATION CUM PARTY FOR THE BAND (EXCEPT WHEN DOWN IN THE HOLE) AND THEN THERE WAS ME, ON A KIND OF MISSION TO BECOME. YOU CAN SEE IN SOME OF THESE SHOTS JUST HOW HAPPY I WAS WITH WHAT I WAS BECOMING, AND HOW BIZARRE WERE THE TWISTS ON ANOTHER SIDE.

ANYWAY, MICK ROCK CAME BY ONE DAY, SENT BY MAINMAN TO SNAP US, AND HE WAS A BREATH OF FRESH AIR. NO PRESSURE, NO AIR OF AUTHORITY, HAPPILY CORRUPTIBLE BUT NOT YET CORRUPTED, A BIG, YOUNG ENGLISH PUPPY WITH A FLOPPY 'FRO AND AN ENTHUSIASM FOR LIFE IN GENERAL AND NOTHING IN PARTICULAR, HAPPY BUT NOT TOO HAPPY, NICE PALE SKIN, ACQUIESCENT… AND YET, THERE WAS SOMETHING ELSE GOING ON… A CERTAIN AUTHORITY IN HIS PHYSICAL HEIGHT; A SHARP INQUISITIVENESS IN THE GAZE, AIDED AND FOCUSED BY THE PROMINENT, POINTY NOSE. HE PUT OUT AN OVERALL IMPRESSION OF GOOD BREEDING THAT PREVENTED HIM PUTTING A FOOT WRONG OR RUINING A SCENE. HE ALSO HAD A FRESHNESS AND TIMELINESS OF BEING.

MY FAVORITES AMONG THESE PICTURES ARE THE IMAGES OF SCOTT ASHETON, WHO JUST PLAIN LOOKS LIKE THE REAL THING. I THINK IT'S HIS DRUMMING THAT PUT OVER THE WHOLE GROUP, REALLY, AND HIS PRESENCE MADE US A CREDIBLE STREET GANG.

OUR TIME IN ENGLAND WAS A REAL EXAMPLE OF THE OLD CLICHÉ OF ARTISTS FORGETTING ALL ELSE AND LIVING FOR THEIR ART – TO REACH A PURIFIED PLANE, BLAH BLAH BLAH; OF COURSE, THIS REALLY IS A DULL OLD SAW AND NO WAY TO GET ALONG IN LIFE, BUT THE GOODS *WERE* GOOD; AND WE WERE COSSETED 'TIL THEIR BIRTH. SO THERE.

FOR THAT I MUST THANK MAINMAN MANAGEMENT, WHO PROTECTED US THAT FAR, AND SENT THE RIGHT GUY ALONG TO SNAP IT ALL UP.

**IGGY POP**
JANUARY 2005

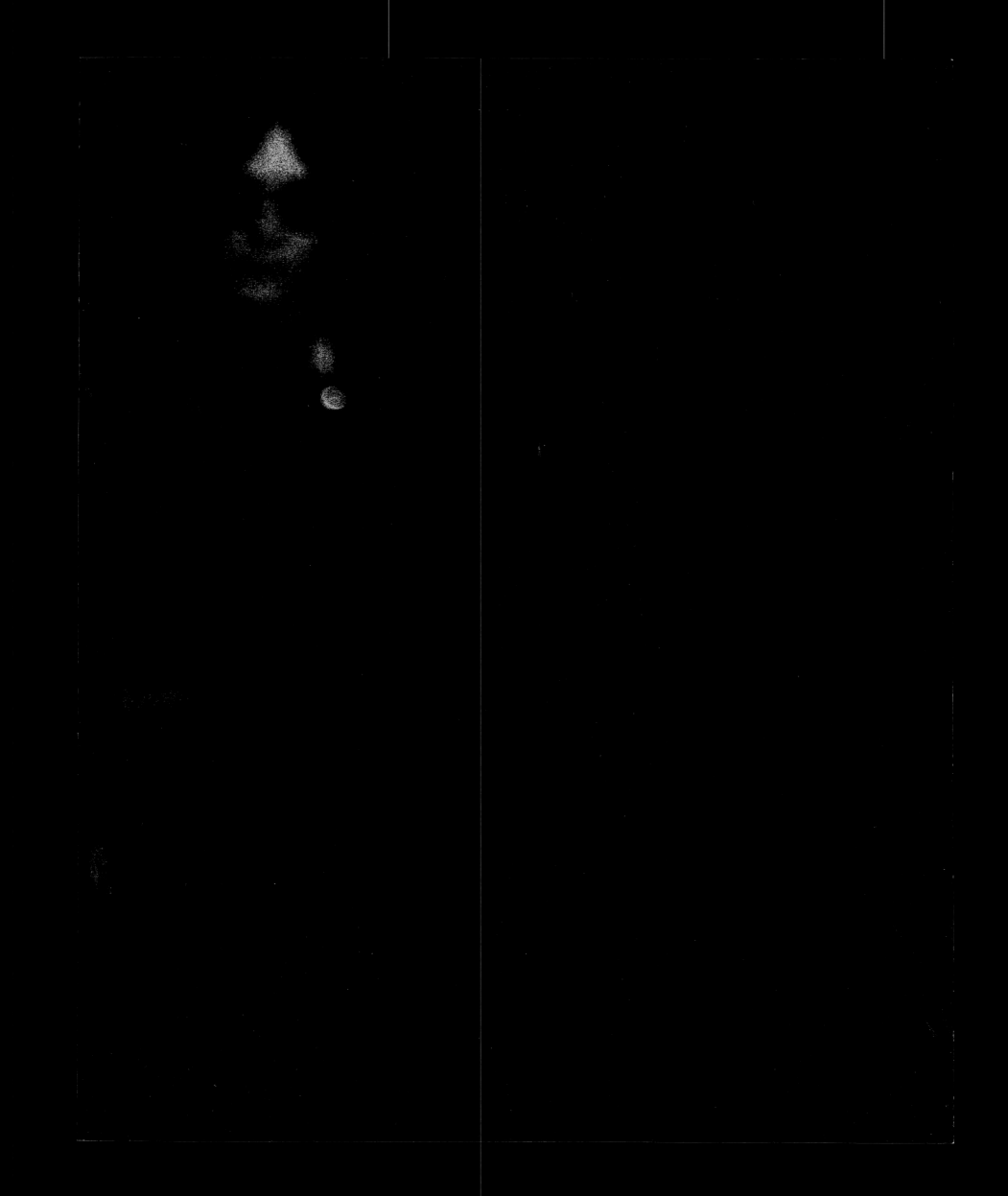

THE SESSION  Thirty-three years is a long time.
It's not always easy to go back. But 1972 was a potent
year for rock n' roll, for London, for me. I saw, (and
photographed), the rise of Ziggy Stardust, Mott The
Hoople's 'All The Young Dudes', the surfacing of Lou
Reed and the Bowie/Mick Ronson produced *Transformer*
(and its key cut 'Walk On The Wild Side') and *Raw Power*
(which wasn't released until 1973, but was recorded,
mixed and photographed in 1972). I don't recall it like
it was yesterday, but I do recall certain shiny moments
in a year that transformed all our lives.

David Bowie introduced me to Jim Osterberg at a welcome party he had organized for Jim's first UK visit at some little veggie restaurant off Westbourne Grove, where everyone sat on the floor, in the early summer of 1972.

David had often riffed enthusiastically to me about the Ig, who in many ways was the inspiration for (Z)iggy Stardust. He swapped tales of Iggy for stories of Syd Barrett, an intimate of mine.

The very informed (and very hip) of London at the time had heard apocalyptic stories of peanut butter, broken glass and blood, and I maybe expected someone of an outrageous, outgoing nature, so I was struck by how quiet, polite, almost shy, Jim was.

Shortly after, I bore witness to the other side of this unique coin at a concert at the recently converted La Scala cinema in King's Cross, the Stooges' one and only show ever in the UK. Even the early albums and the tales of gore hadn't prepared me (or any of us). Remember this 1972 (although the Stooges in some form had been on and off the game since 1967). A rock n' roll lifetime before the advent of the Sex Pistols and 'Punk Rock'. For a London lad this was an unprecedented experience.

I remember feeling distinctly intimidated, even as I boldly aimed my lens at him. He appeared so much bigger in the frame that I knew him to be. He had undergone a complete and dangerous transformation, and I was totally fascinated. Little did I comprehend how great a resonance the images I was collecting would have. How could any of us have known the legendary status this concert would attain.

It seemed to last a lifetime (although it was in fact only 40 minutes) and it changed everything. There was no blood and broken glass, but we were all riveted and devastated by the ritual enacted before us.

Never was there a truer description – 'Raw Power!'

A couple of weeks later Iggy's manager Tony Defries (also Bowie's manager) called me. Two or three publications needed recent Stooges pics en groupe and there were none. It wasn't a commission (nor was the King's Cross session). Tony didn't believe in paying for photographs. But he understood my enthusiasm and my naivete, and knew that I would jump at the opportunity (which I did). In those days I came very cheap (I even paid all expenses). In truth, nobody valued rock photography very highly at the time. But I didn't care. I got my kicks out of aiming my lens; everything else was unimportant and my material needs were modest.

I had one camera and two lenses (a normal and a wide angle) and my red sneakers, and I was flying. It took me a while to locate the trashed out basement rehearsal studio off the Fulham Road, but I was buzzed. I had tracked the Stooges to their lair, and they were to be mine for a whole hour! There was no brief. There never was in those days. Just grab a fistful of frames and get out. But it was my nature to linger and probe around, to cram as much variety as I could into a few modest rolls of film. And in fact, the Stooges were glad to see me.

They were bored with rehearsing for the upcoming

*Raw Power* recording sessions, and I provided respite and distraction. It wasn't as if they were inundated by attention, or local photographers kicking down the door desperate to immortalize them! Those were very different times and there were few shutterbugs on the music scene. I was the only one who shot them on their *Raw Power* jaunt.

First, I recorded the Stooges as a group, then later individually (which, of course, meant mostly Iggy). They were very cooperative, and I remember it was Iggy's idea to be shot embracing the toilet bowl! Iggy and Ron Asheton were communicative although James Williamson was the most voluble, while Scott Asheton hardly mumbled a note.

I remember James explaining to me that the Stooges' attention could wander easily, and not linger too long with one set-up: a hint I readily took. Certainly the location and circumstances were ideal for the Stooges. I worked with the available light (3 or 4 bare light bulbs hanging from the ceiling) and a long exposure or a small flash on the camera. 'Raw' was what we got and it was of course perfect. As I always did in those early years, I processed all the black and white photos myself.

Some of the negatives are even somewhat fogged. Who knows why, but that only seems to add to the overall flavour.

A key point to note is that none of these photos (King's Cross or the basement) were shot with an album package in mind, and of course the Stooges hadn't even begun to record. The decision to use them came a few months later in New York where I was lensing Ziggy Stardust's first US tour, when CBS decided they wanted Bowie to remix the album and to release it in early 1973. Since these were the only recent photos available, out of necessity they made the grade. In their largesse, CBS even paid me a couple of hundred dollars! And I'm sure I was grateful for the pittance! It was great to be young and not give a damn about such trivial matters as geld.

The beauty of it all is that as copyright owner of these images — which have become an indelible part of rock 'n' roll lore, my naivete has been rewarded many times over in the years in-between.

Time and again life has proven itself to be wild and unpredictable, I'm grateful to say.

"The visionary artist inhabits the eye of the hurricane.
For him chaos is both inspiration and balm for his turbulent soul."

Villiers de L'Isle Adam, 1881

TAKEN FROM AN INTERVIEW WITH IGGY POP CONDUCTED BY MICK ROCK IN THE SUMMER OF 1972 BEFORE THE RECORDING OF *RAW POWER*

**DEATH TRIP** Iggy Pop is, you might say, extreme. He makes the Mick Jaggers and Alice Coopers of this world look kind of timid. Words such as 'spontaneous' and 'unpredictable', frequently applied to him, are a little short on power. Iggy is a monster.

*Rock* magazines have spewed out reams of literature dedicated to the propagation of the Iggy legend. *"Yes"*, he modestly admits, *"I'm a legendary figure, I am strangely enough."* He's never cared much for what's been written about him, but he likes the fact that it's been written. *"I like being news"*. He likes to shock although that's only a side product of what his trip is about.

Iggy's exploits are not for the delectation of the faint-hearted. He has trodden where no one else has yet dared. Tales of gore, of ripping flesh, crushed bones, shattered teeth, of hat wax poured over naked torsos, of frothing obscenities, of dark insanities enacted to the bloodthirsty whelps and gurgles of a voice which sounds as if it's just crawled out of the primordial slime … All this and Iggy says, *"I consider my music very understated. I only really just hint around the edges of what I'm into."* Now supposing he got just a little carried away one night…?

I consider my my music very understated

I only really just hint hint around the edges of what I'm into

I'm a legendary figure
I am strangely enough

I like being news.

**GIMME DANGER** *"People hear about all these things I've done; they get the wrong impression."* Why, aren't they true? *"Sure, they're true. Its just things I get into from time to time. It's like you're around for a while and things happen. I smash my mouth a little on the mike, get a little knocked about by the audience, people think it happens all the time."*

One night, stone-drunk, he vomited all over the first couple of rows at Ungarno's Club in New York. One of his favourite antics is to leap off the stage into the crowd, and thrash about like a landed fish, daring them to, well, do things to him. Some American audiences don't need much encouragement. There was the time some of this activity got shown on the TV. *"I was held down, while one chick was pullin' off my pants, some others were tryin' to French kiss me. And this other one gave me a blowjob. All the while I'd be kickin' one, hittin' another. I like to fight chicks off. It turns me on. I like violence. Strange chicks...although I'm not really very violent."* And it may be true; off stage it's amazing to realize just how small Iggy is. In performance, he projects a gargantuan persona, doing back bends and somersaults and assorted bodily contortions of a kind which would stir even an advanced yogi from a trance. *"I'm jus' doin' my part."* He struts about with an aura of total arrogance and defiance when on stage. *"But how do I know what I look like? I look at photos, sure, but it never looks like me. I just like to be up there. I like bein' on stage. It's the only time I feel really calm, nice. I jus' gotten used to havin' my own way."* For years he's done pretty much what he wanted to, on and off stage. *"It gets hard to change. You get used to not bein' a nice guy."* He has a very existential attitude towards his audience: he's not about to play the modern bourgeois pop star for them. *"I jus' got this band and if anyone wants to see it, they can pay and get in and I'm trying' hard to do a good show. I'm givin' it everything I've got."* And that would be hard to deny. *"But I ain't gonna be patronizing,"* he snarls. *"I'm sick of all this crap about ovations, and how many encores. I tell ya, when I'm into a band, I can't even take time out to clap."*

I was held down, w
pullin' off my pants
tryin' to French kis
one gave me a blow
I'd be kickin' one.
I like to fight chick
I like violence. Stra
I'm not really very

ile one chick was
some others were
me. And this other
ob. All the while
ttin' another.
off. It turns me on.
ge chicks...although
iolent.

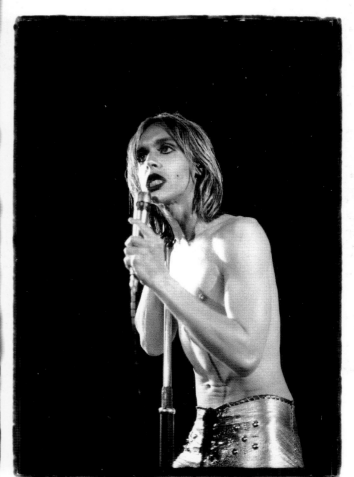

**SEARCH AND DESTROY** When I saw him recently in London at The Scala in Kings Cross, he spent some time wandering round the audience talking about wanting to find something 'interesting'.

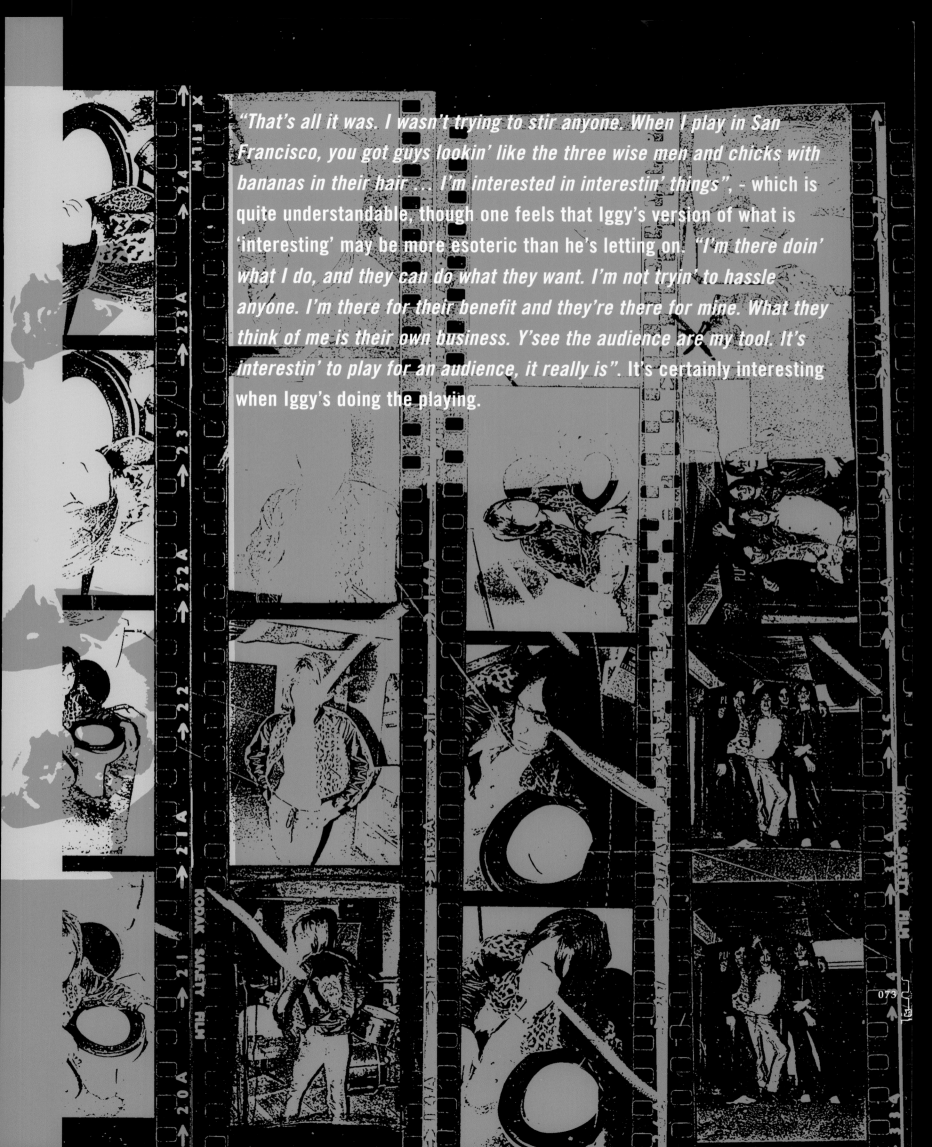

"That's all it was. I wasn't trying to stir anyone. When I play in San Francisco, you got guys lookin' like the three wise men and chicks with bananas in their hair ... I'm interested in interestin' things", - which is quite understandable, though one feels that Iggy's version of what is 'interesting' may be more esoteric than he's letting on. "I'm there doin' what I do, and they can do what they want. I'm not tryin' to hassle anyone. I'm there for their benefit and they're there for mine. What they think of me is their own business. Y'see the audience are my tool. It's interestin' to play for an audience, it really is". It's certainly interesting when Iggy's doing the playing.

I'm there doi
and they can
want. I'm not
hassle anyone
for their bene
they're there

what I do.
do what they
tryin' to
I'm there
fit and
or mine.

**RAW POWER** Iggy's band is called the Stooges. It started off as the Psychedelic Stooges. Something about an acid trip and an old film of the Three Stooges. Elektra Records made them crop the psychedelic part for their first album. Some silly notion of it being too provocative.

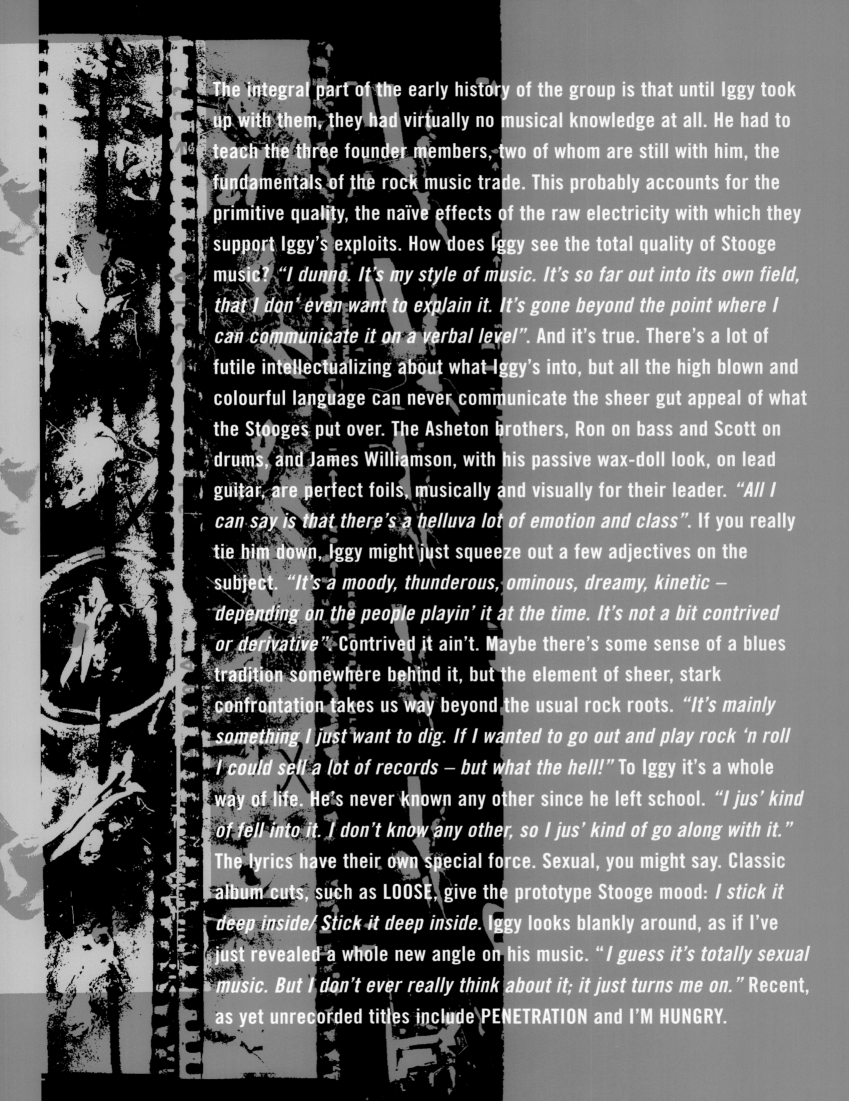

The integral part of the early history of the group is that until Iggy took up with them, they had virtually no musical knowledge at all. He had to teach the three founder members, two of whom are still with him, the fundamentals of the rock music trade. This probably accounts for the primitive quality, the naïve effects of the raw electricity with which they support Iggy's exploits. How does Iggy see the total quality of Stooge music? *"I dunno. It's my style of music. It's so far out into its own field, that I don' even want to explain it. It's gone beyond the point where I can communicate it on a verbal level"*. And it's true. There's a lot of futile intellectualizing about what Iggy's into, but all the high blown and colourful language can never communicate the sheer gut appeal of what the Stooges put over. The Asheton brothers, Ron on bass and Scott on drums, and James Williamson, with his passive wax-doll look, on lead guitar, are perfect foils, musically and visually for their leader. *"All I can say is that there's a helluva lot of emotion and class"*. If you really tie him down, Iggy might just squeeze out a few adjectives on the subject. *"It's a moody, thunderous, ominous, dreamy, kinetic — depending on the people playin' it at the time. It's not a bit contrived or derivative".* Contrived it ain't. Maybe there's some sense of a blues tradition somewhere behind it, but the element of sheer, stark confrontation takes us way beyond the usual rock roots. *"It's mainly something I just want to dig. If I wanted to go out and play rock 'n roll I could sell a lot of records — but what the hell!"* To Iggy it's a whole way of life. He's never known any other since he left school. *"I jus' kind of fell into it. I don't know any other, so I jus' kind of go along with it."* The lyrics have their own special force. Sexual, you might say. Classic album cuts, such as **LOOSE**, give the prototype Stooge mood: *I stick it deep inside/ Stick it deep inside.* Iggy looks blankly around, as if I've just revealed a whole new angle on his music. *"I guess it's totally sexual music. But I don't ever really think about it; it just turns me on."* Recent, as yet unrecorded titles include **PENETRATION** and **I'M HUNGRY**.

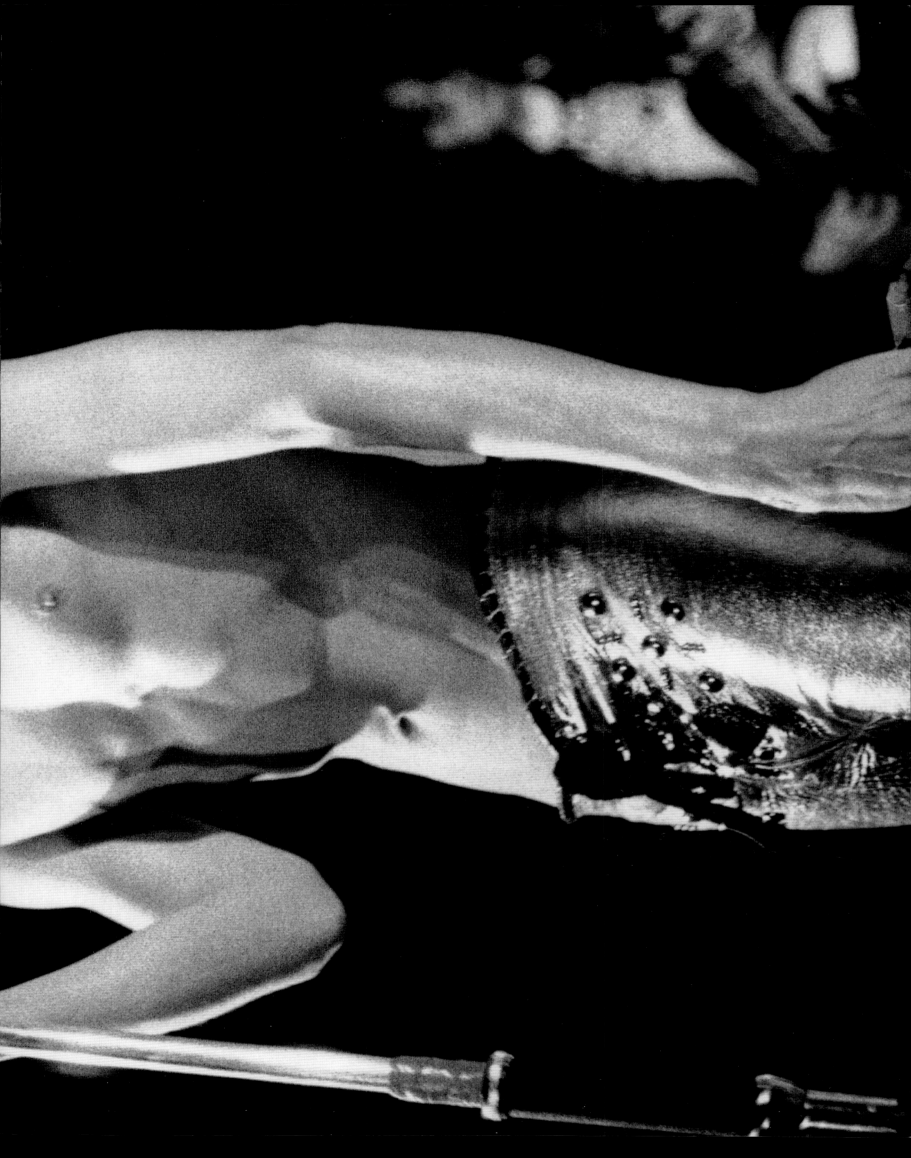

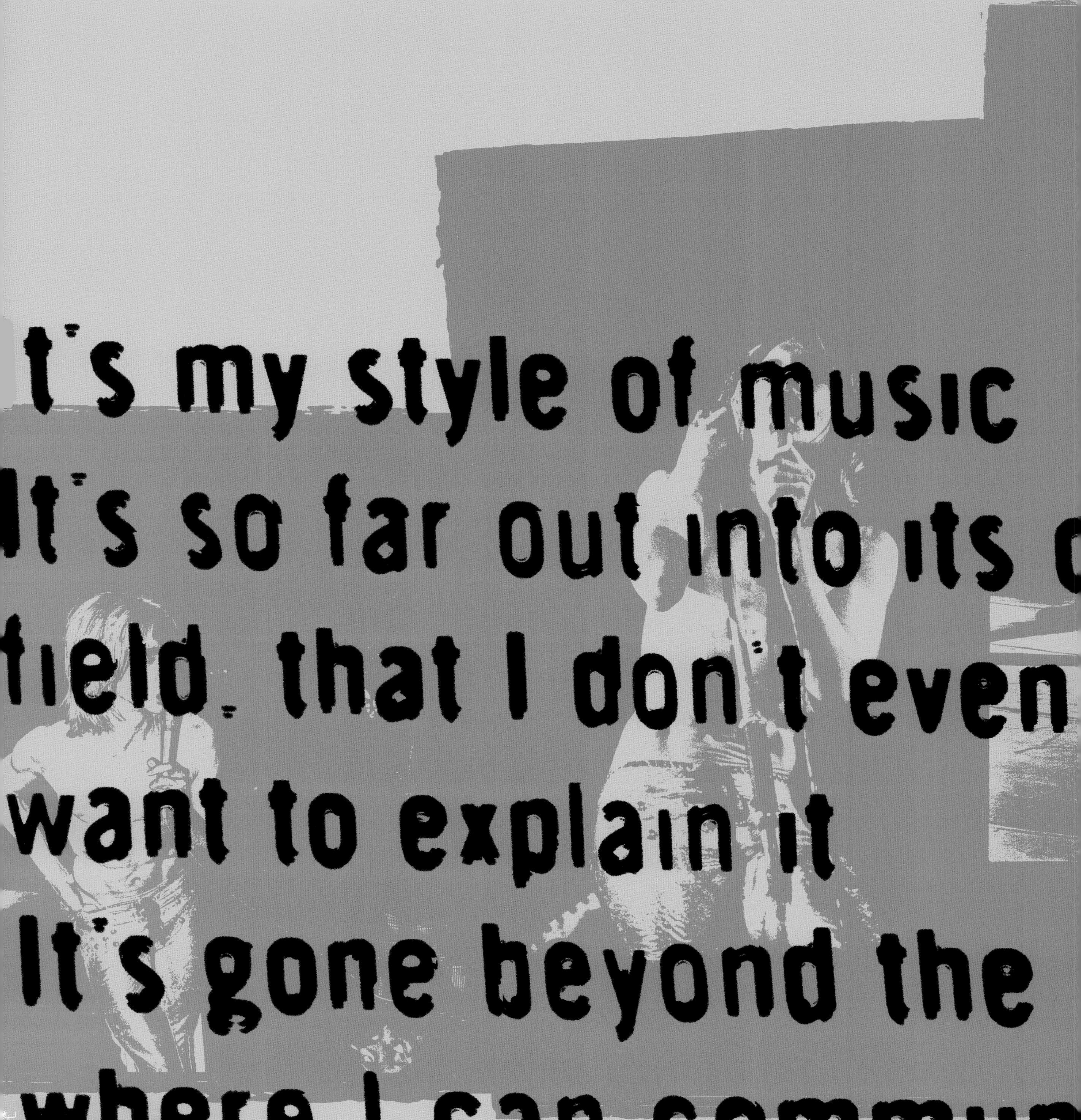

It's my style of music
It's so far out into its o
field. that I don't even
want to explain it
It's gone beyond the
where I can commun
it on a verbal level

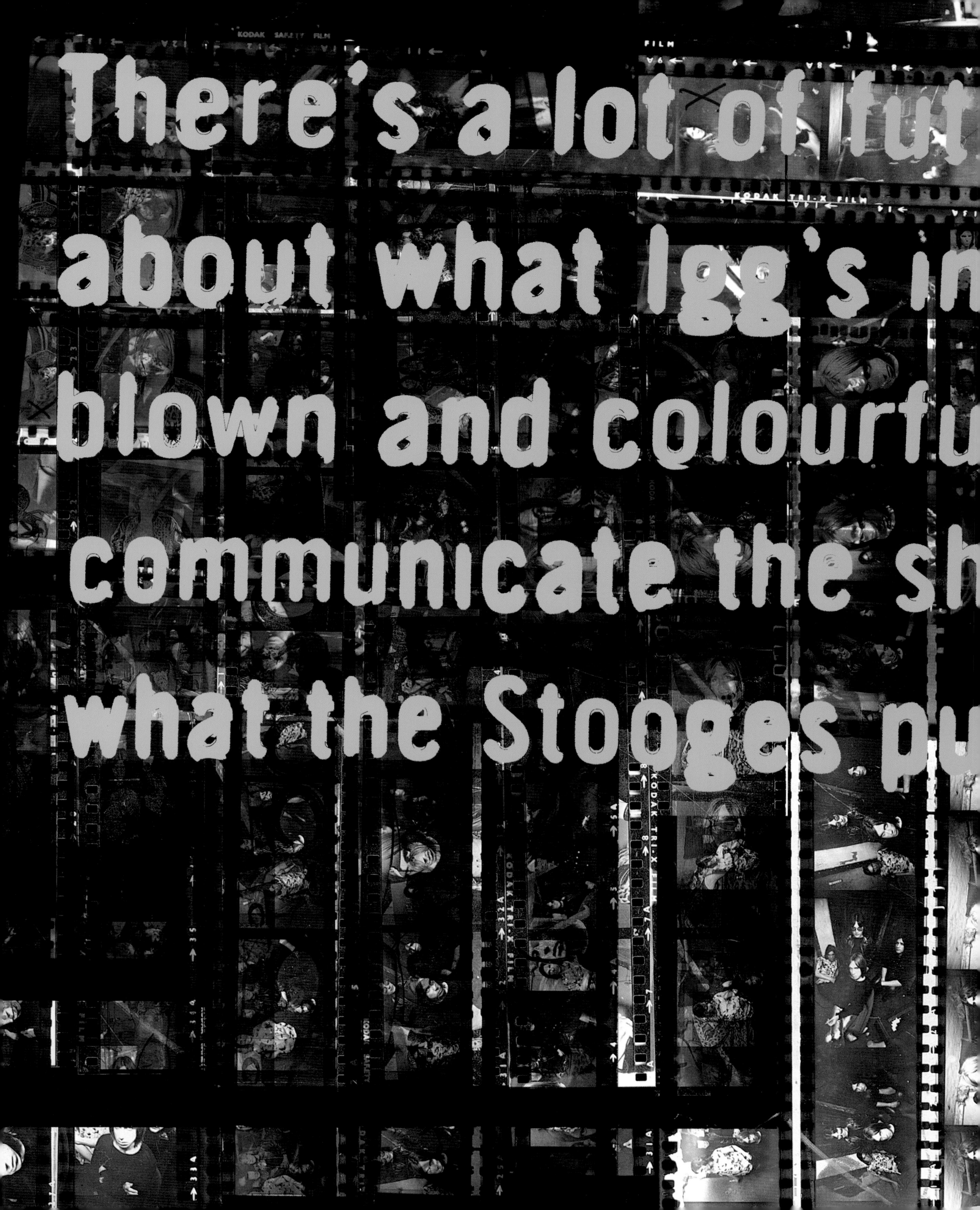

There's a lot of fu

about what Igg's in

blown and colourfu

communicate the sh

what the Stooges pu

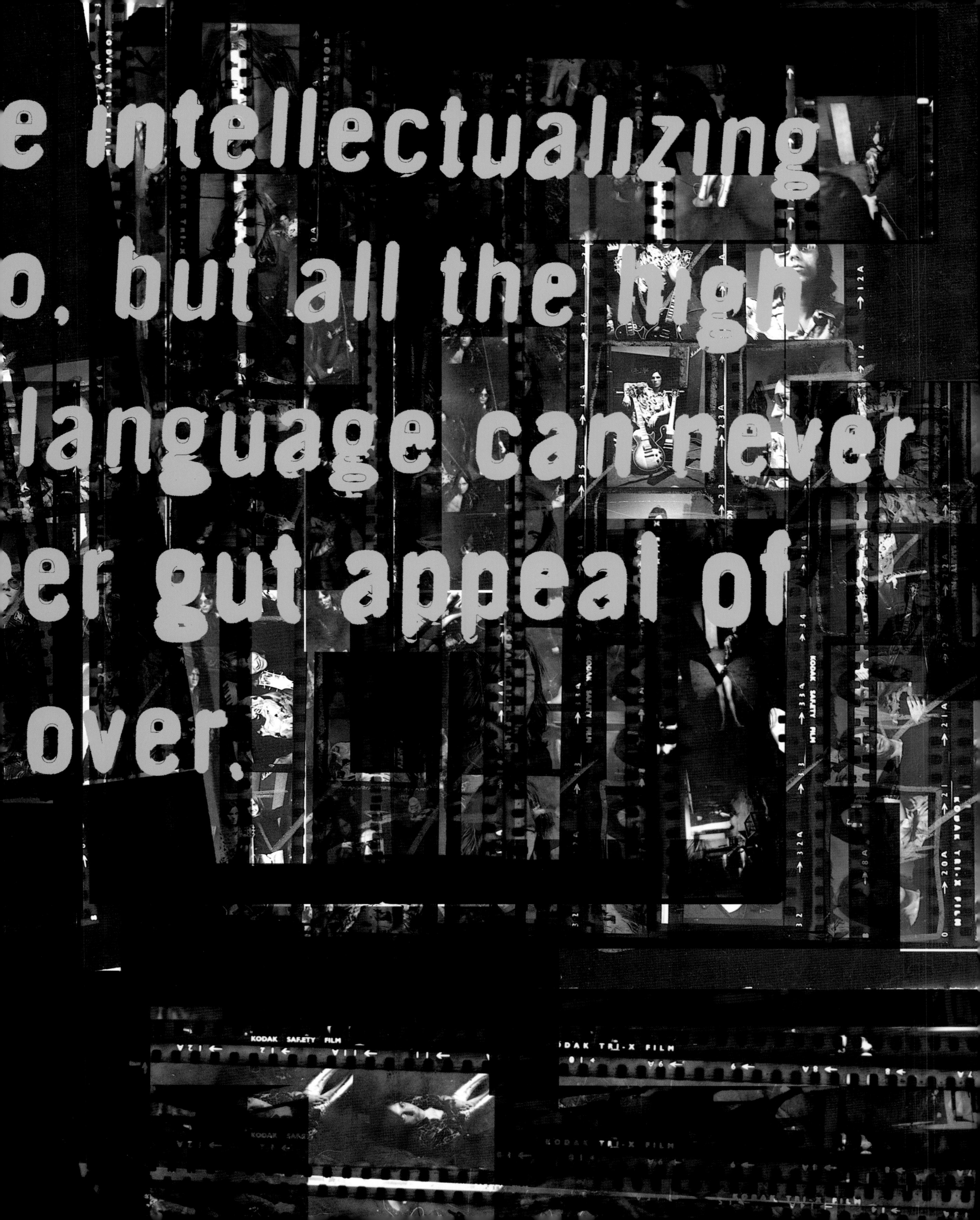

e intellectualizing

o, but all the high

language can never

er gut appeal of

over.

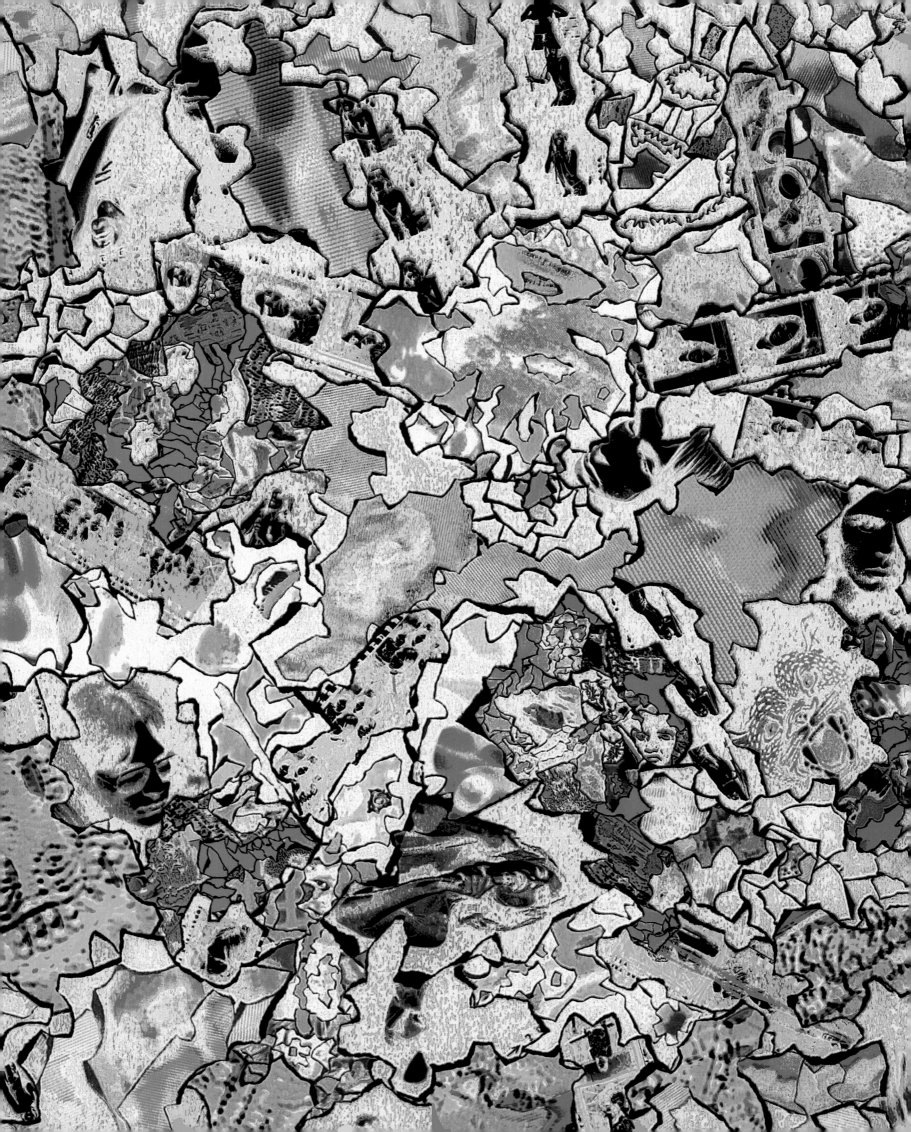

TAKEN FROM AN INTERVIEW WITH IGGY POP CONDUCTED BY MICK ROCK IN THE SUMMER OF 1972 BEFORE THE RECORDING OF *RAW POWER*

# PENETRATION Strange to relate, Iggy says he doesn't have a very strong sex drive.

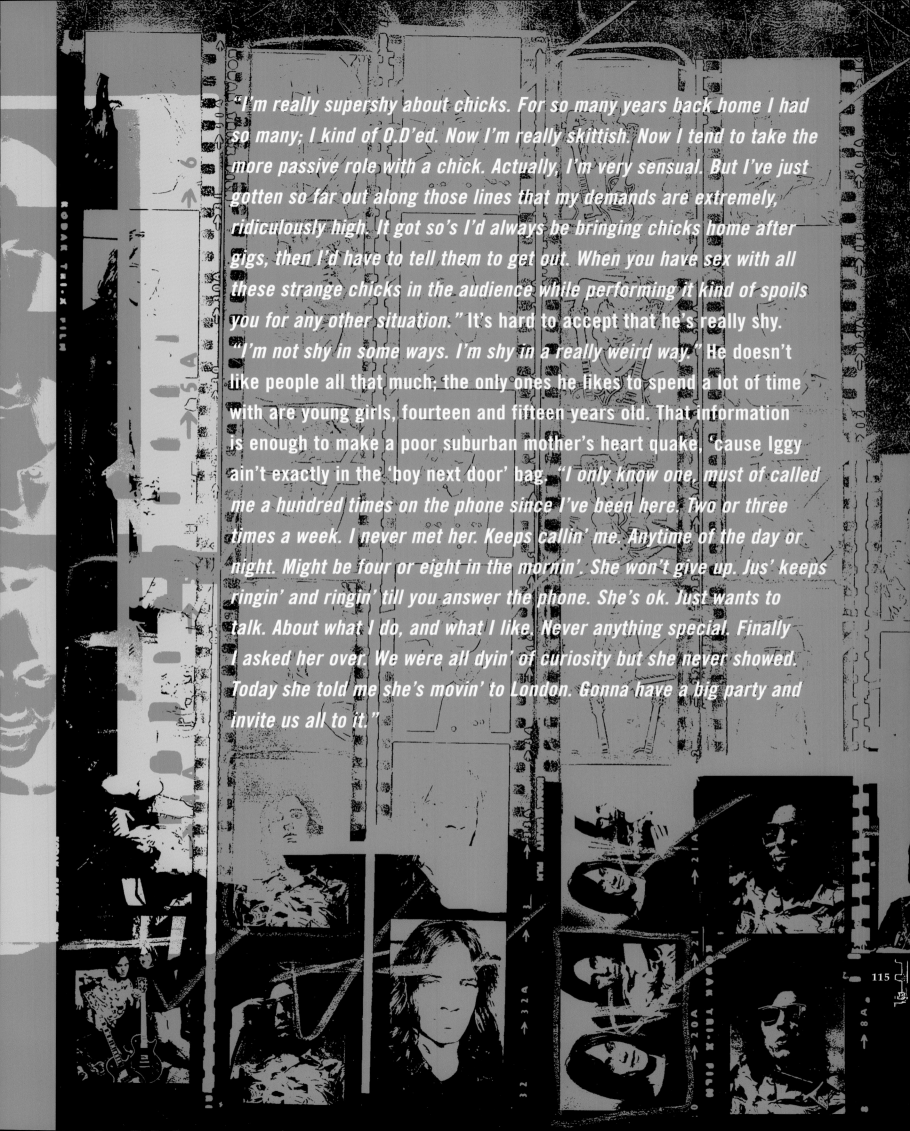

"I'm really supershy about chicks. For so many years back home I had so many; I kind of O.D'ed. Now I'm really skittish. Now I tend to take the more passive role with a chick. Actually, I'm very sensual. But I've just gotten so far out along those lines that my demands are extremely, ridiculously high. It got so's I'd always be bringing chicks home after gigs, then I'd have to tell them to get out. When you have sex with all these strange chicks in the audience while performing it kind of spoils you for any other situation." It's hard to accept that he's really shy. "I'm not shy in some ways. I'm shy in a really weird way." He doesn't like people all that much; the only ones he likes to spend a lot of time with are young girls, fourteen and fifteen years old. That information is enough to make a poor suburban mother's heart quake, 'cause Iggy ain't exactly in the 'boy next door' bag. "I only know one, must of called me a hundred times on the phone since I've been here. Two or three times a week. I never met her. Keeps callin' me. Anytime of the day or night. Might be four or eight in the mornin'. She won't give up. Jus' keeps ringin' and ringin' till you answer the phone. She's ok. Just wants to talk. About what I do, and what I like. Never anything special. Finally I asked her over. We were all dyin' of curiosity but she never showed. Today she told me she's movin' to London. Gonna have a big party and invite us all to it."

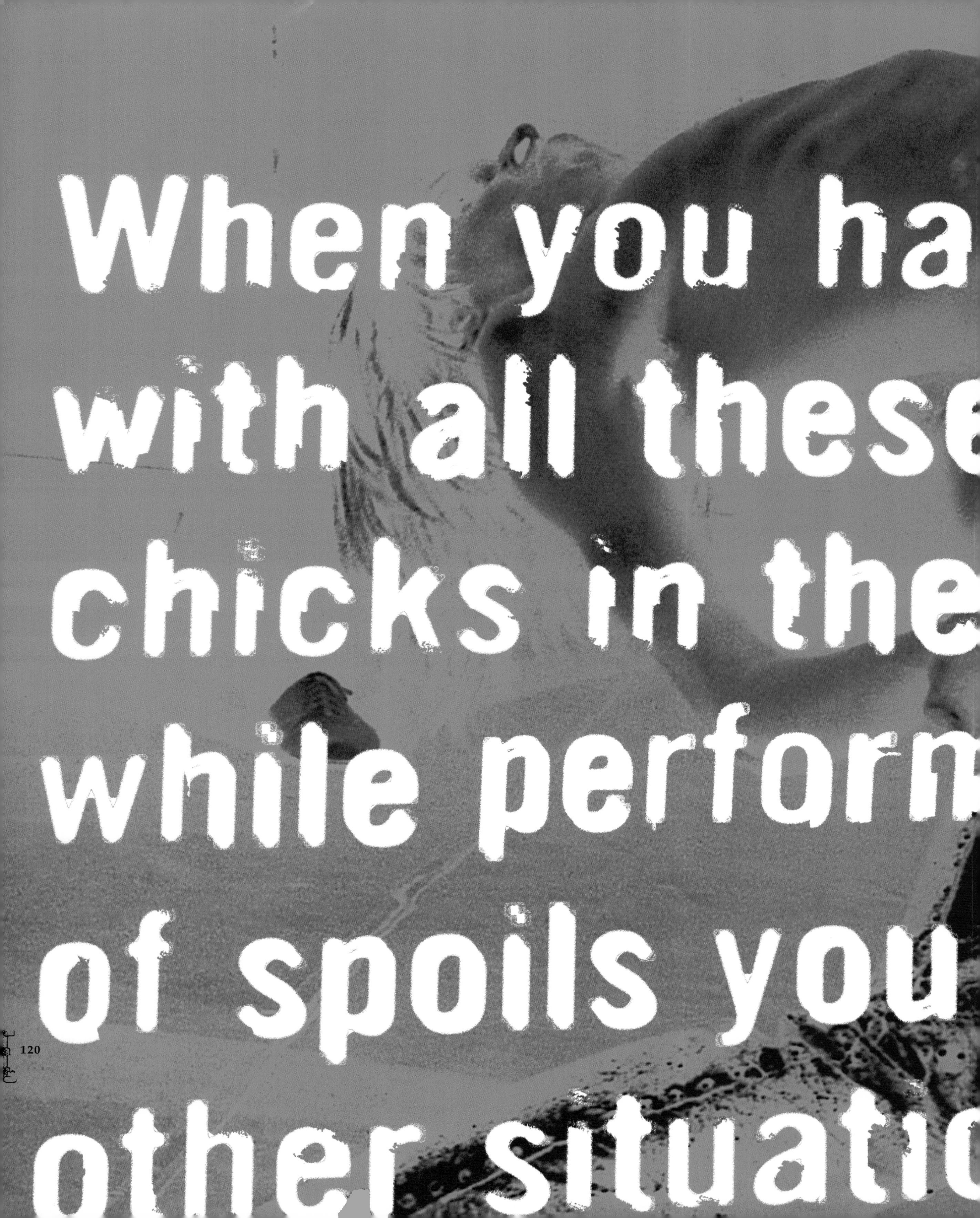

When you ha
with all these
chicks in the
while perforn
of spoils you
other situatio

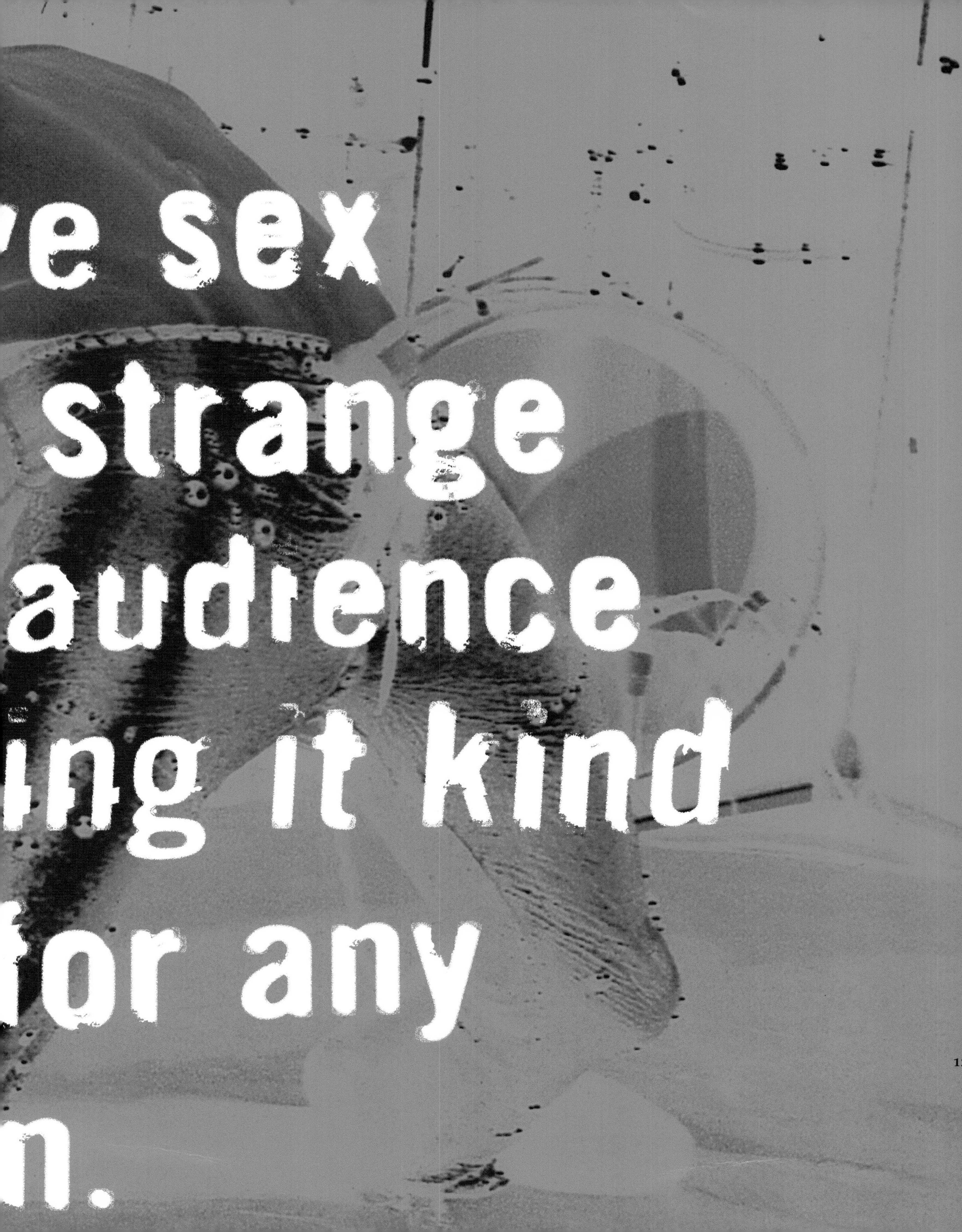

ve sex
strange
audience
ing it kind
or any
n.

Iggy Pop is Iggy Pop and that's final.

TAKEN FROM AN INTERVIEW WITH IGGY POP CONDUCTED BY MICK ROCK IN THE SUMMER OF 1972 BEFORE THE RECORDING OF *RAW POWER*

**I NEED SOMEBODY** He spends most of his time on his own, when he's not working with the band. He sleeps a lot. Often he won't answer the door to visitors. *"I have a kind of reclusive personality."* This idea doesn't fit in too well with his public image. *"No, well, of necessity when I do time around people I get it in big doses. It's not that I don't like knowin' people. I jus' don' like them getting too intimate."*

Iggy has known more audience familiarity than any other stage performer, past or present. And it can't be said that he doesn't encourage it. Iggy acquired his notable identity tag when playing with a small town Michigan band called the Iguanas. Iggy is a diminutive of Iguana, in case you hadn't registered. For a time he was Iggy Stooge. Now he prefers Iggy Pop. Pop is an adaptation of Popp, the surname of an old friend of his. He no longer answers to the name he was born with – he left that skin behind him long ago. *"Pop is my real name now. The other is my parents'. I don't like all this confusion about names. I like Iggy Pop. It suits me."* Iggy Pop is Iggy Pop and that's final.

His recent London performance was his first public appearance in eighteen months. There was a very good reason for this lay off. *"I was pretty sick. I've been comin' off a year of drug addiction. Very heavily into it. It ain't easy comin' off."* He's completely clean now.

Understandably not the kind of man to have much faith in institutions, he didn't go to any clinic for help. He got himself off. *"It's hard to explain how I got into it. But I wouldn't recommend it."* That's what mainly brought him to England. After he'd got himself over the worst stage of withdrawal, he decided he wanted to stay away from his old haunts while he got himself together again. But he wants to go back as soon as he feels ready. *"England's very different to what I'm used to, very slowed down. I'm super-homesick for New York, Miami, or even Detroit. Y'know, the ocean, goin' to a movie late at night. It's not jus' cars and stuff, it's the feel. The feel over here's real weird. It's sort of a matter of what you're used to."* And what Iggy's used to is a far cry from the quiet respectable little street in South Kensington he's been domiciled in for the last six months. Not that he's down on London. He had a good time at the gig...

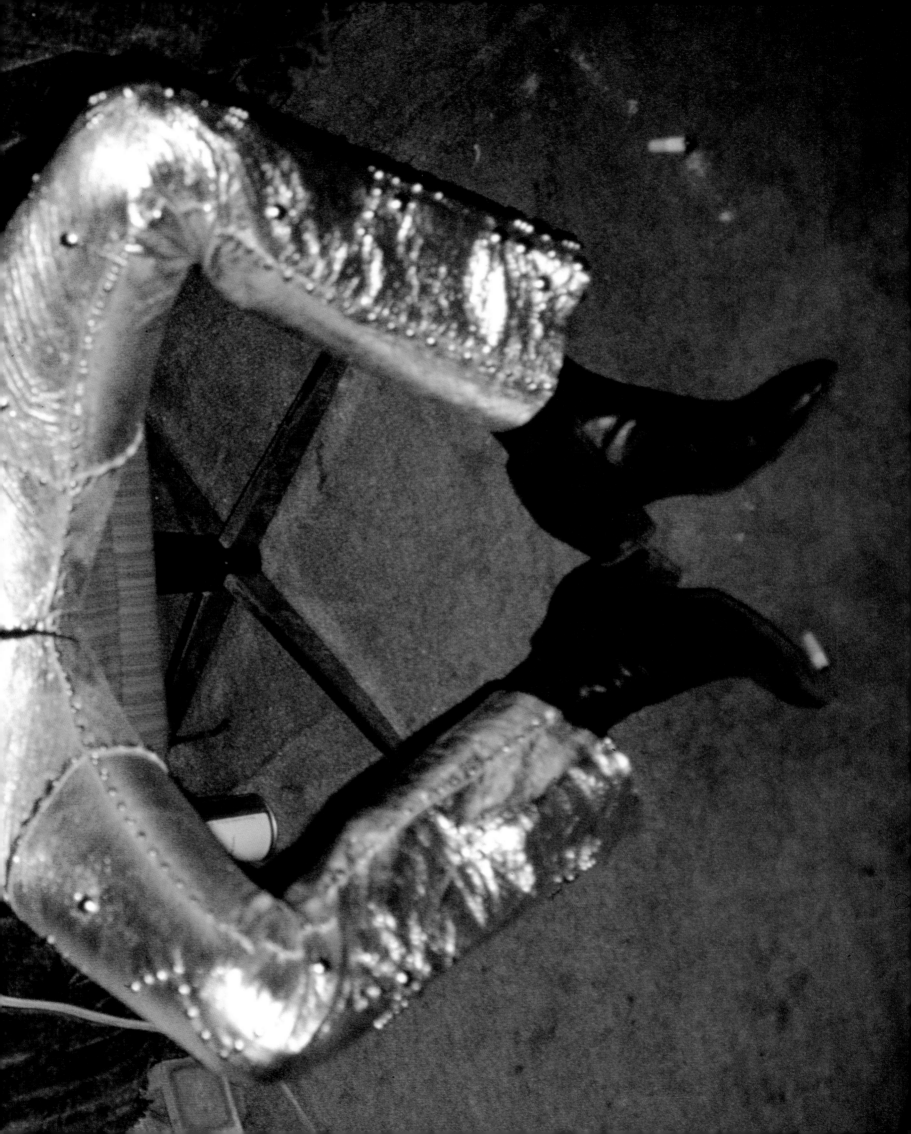

TAKEN FROM AN INTERVIEW WITH IGGY POP CONDUCTED BY MICK ROCK IN THE SUMMER OF 1972 BEFORE THE RECORDING OF *RAW POWER*

# YOUR PRETTY FACE IS GOING TO HELL

The time out hasn't sapped any of his confidence. He explodes like some space age lion onto the largely unsuspecting audience. I mean, reading about Iggy's one thing, seeing him in the flesh is, well, frightening almost. You get the feeling that with him there are no limits – it'll all go just as far as the mood takes him. Nothing is preconceived – except his dress.

Storming onto stage like some skinny freaked-out clockwork doll, arms and legs flailing about as if they had nothing to do with the rest of him, he is dressed only in silver lame, studded trousers, worn as tight as a second skin, and black pointed boots – now there's something for the sentimentalists. His hair is sprayed silver, and thick black makeup encircles his manically glowing eyes. He shakes and rages and falls and crawls and slithers and moans, gurgles, growls, curses, while behind him his band stonily launch their electric gut-assault on the startled freaks who've come to find out… It's so frontal, so basic, that everyone is rigid.

You can't really dance to the Stooges; you just get kind of blown over by them. After lurching and prowling and stumbling over every inch of the stage in the first two numbers, Iggy decides to explore the darkness beyond. He prowls and peers, followed where possible by spotlight, stopping sometimes to stare deep into people's eyes, maybe to drop into some guy's lap and put his arm around him. At one point, he seizes a girl by the hair. She makes no protest; just gazes wide-eyed at her assailant. *I've been hurt but I don't care/I bin dirt but I don't care.* He's dirt, and he don't care, and no mistake. To Iggy, *"People are jus' livin' entertainment. I never stop to think what it's all about."* And he has fun, his way. Those more practiced in the art of Iggy-watching tell me that this night is a particularly subdued one by his own psychotically wild standards. There's no blood or vomit. It's kind of like a workout; just feeling his way back into the old rhythm. Iggy himself enjoyed it in its own way. *"Yeah. Pretty cool. That was one sort of audience. They seemed a bit older. I'd like to sample a real teen audience. I saw a lotta nice girls in the audience. I see beautiful chicks walkin' around London, but I never seem to meet any."* Maybe it's like he said: he's got very high standards.

"I like an art that shrieks its name."

Walter Pater, 1879

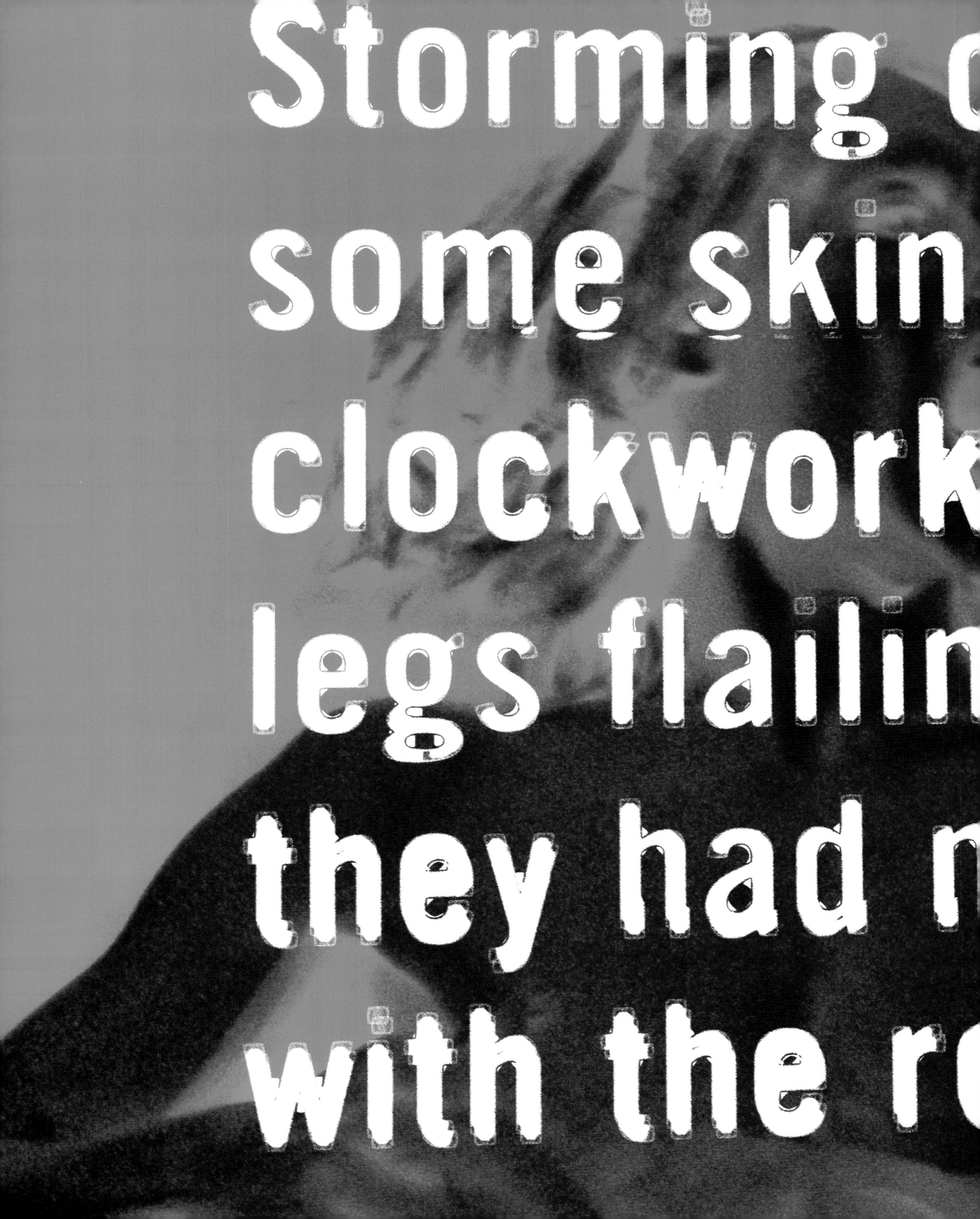

Storming o
some skin
clockwork
legs flailin
they had n
with the re

nto stage like

y freaked-out

doll, arms and

g about as if

othing to do

st of him.

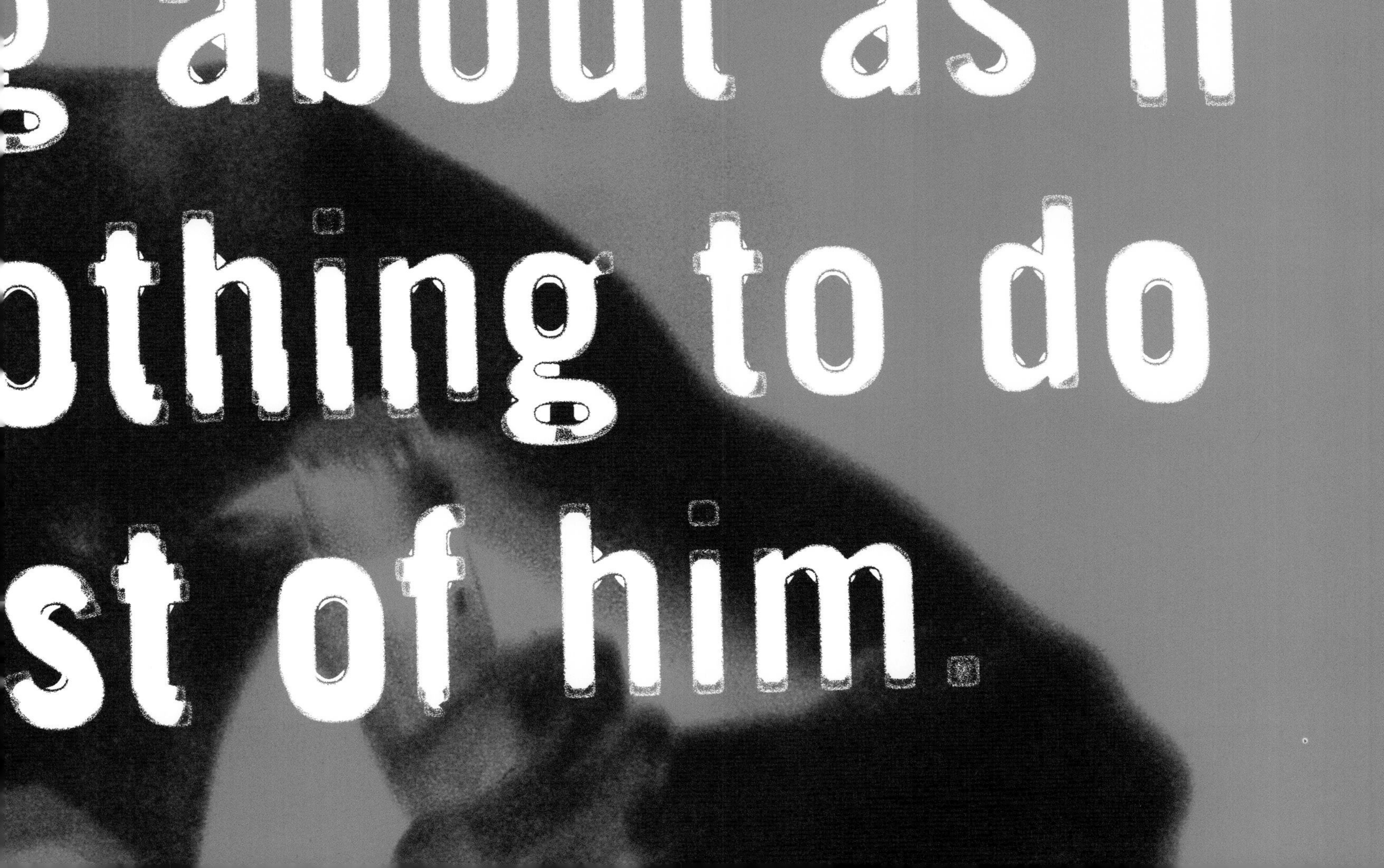

People are just
livin' entertainme

I never stop to th
what it's all about

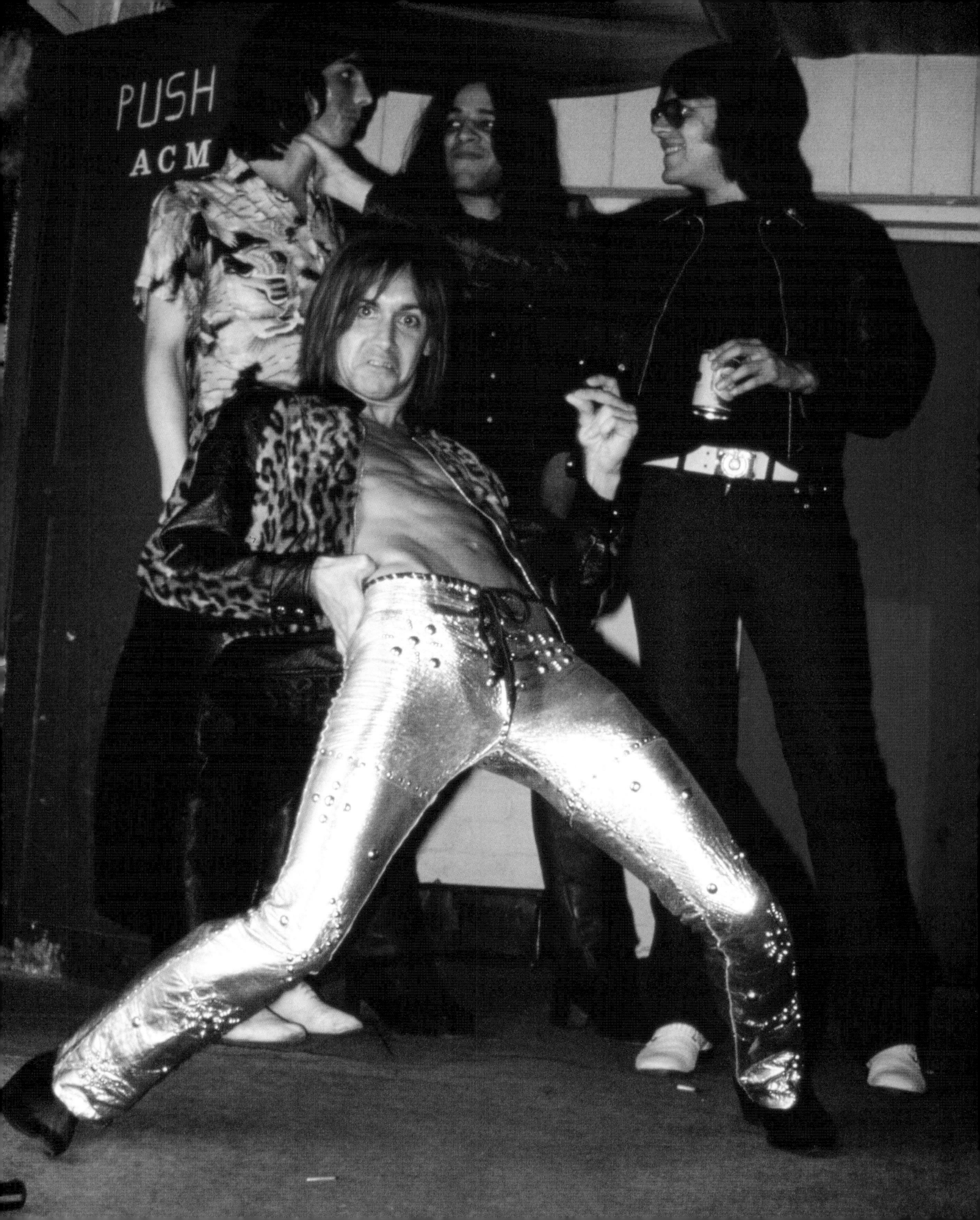
PUSH
ACM

TAKEN FROM AN INTERVIEW WITH IGGY POP CONDUCTED BY MICK ROCK IN THE SUMMER OF 1972 BEFORE THE RECORDING OF *RAW POWER*

**SHAKE APPEAL** This applies also to his musical taste. *"I like the Stones. An' I craved the Doors at one time. Morrison. A big influence. I like lots of pieces of ethnic music. But there's really little that's bein' made now that I really dig. Ninety per cent of it is just a bunch of fake shit."*

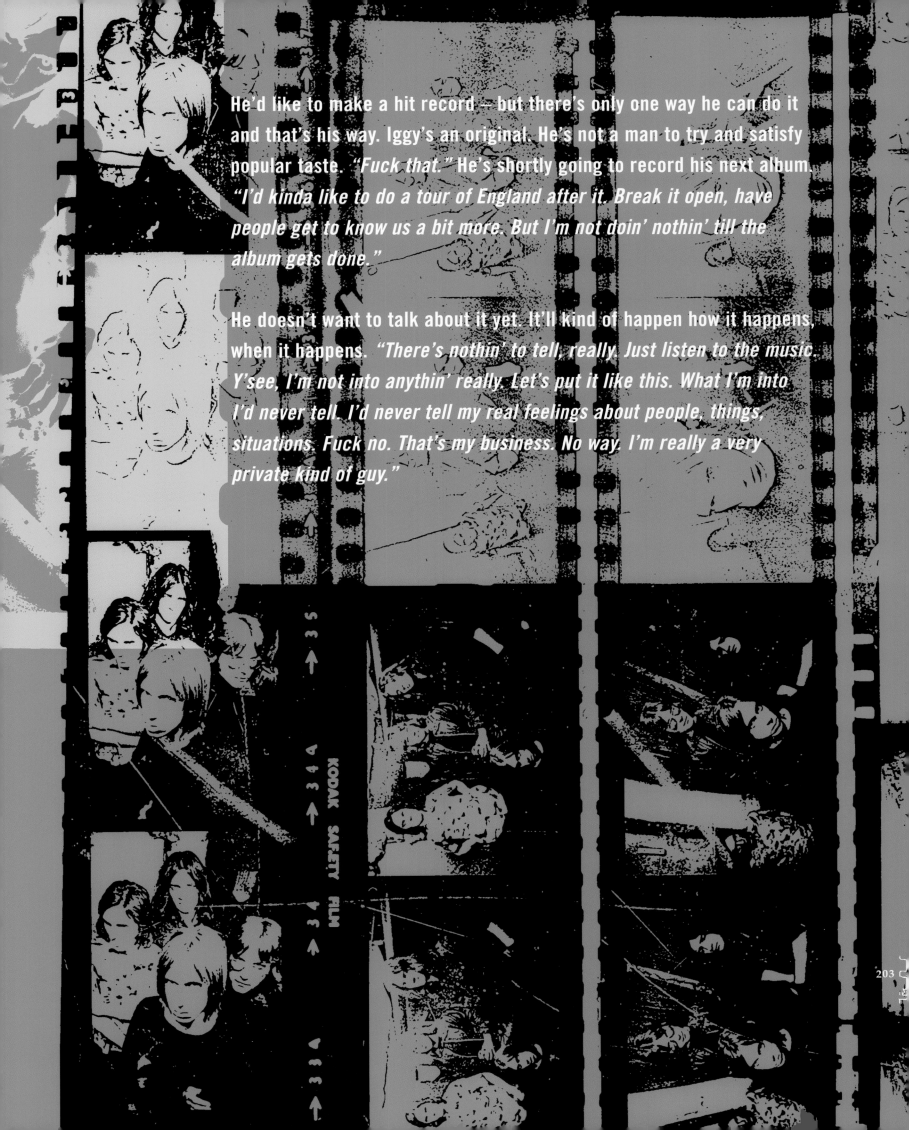

He'd like to make a hit record – but there's only one way he can do it and that's his way. Iggy's an original. He's not a man to try and satisfy popular taste. *"Fuck that."* He's shortly going to record his next album. *"I'd kinda like to do a tour of England after it. Break it open, have people get to know us a bit more. But I'm not doin' nothin' till the album gets done."*

He doesn't want to talk about it yet. It'll kind of happen how it happens, when it happens. *"There's nothin' to tell, really. Just listen to the music. Y'see, I'm not into anythin' really. Let's put it like this. What I'm into I'd never tell. I'd never tell my real feelings about people, things, situations. Fuck no. That's my business. No way. I'm really a very private kind of guy."*

203

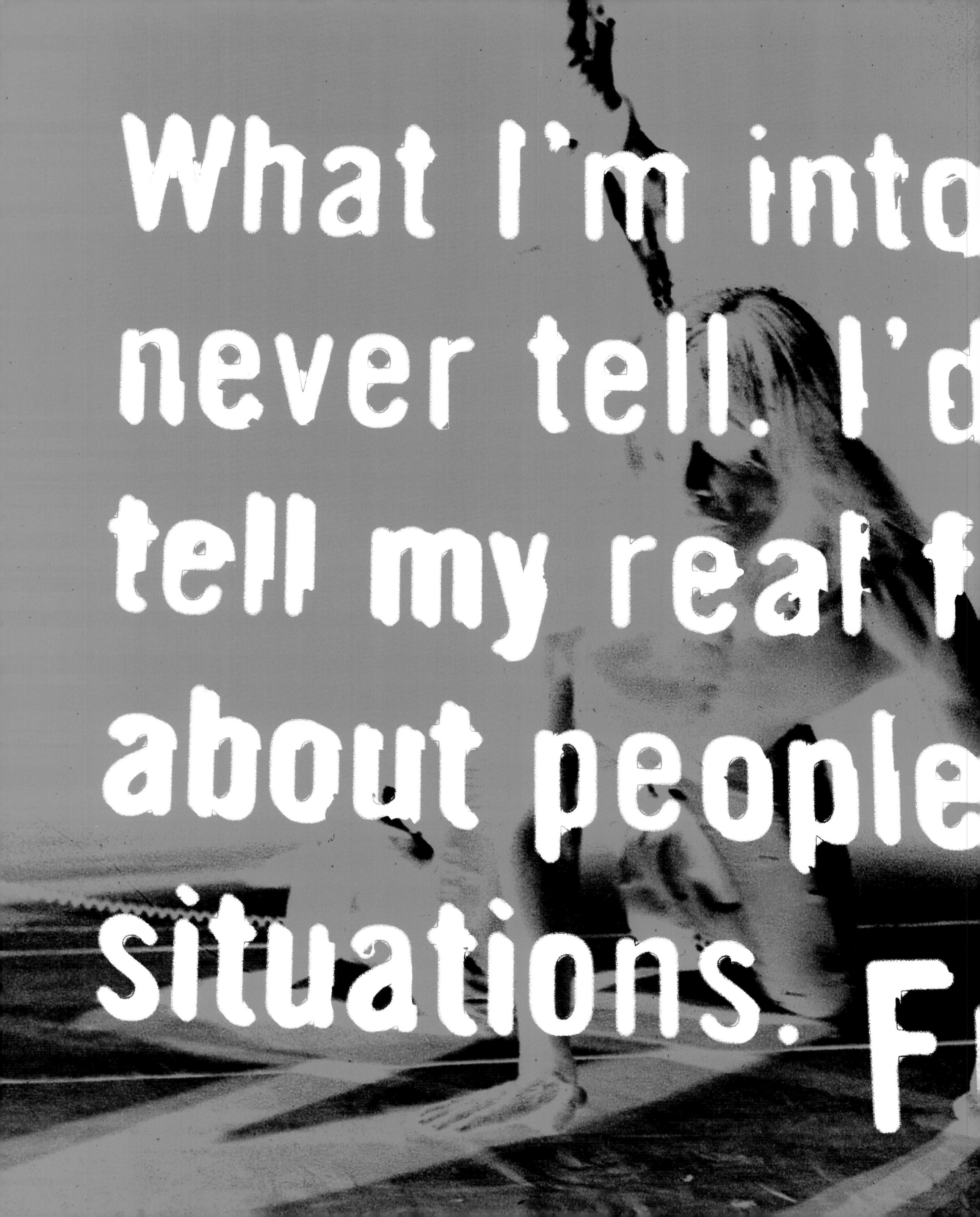

What I'm into
never tell. I'd
tell my real f
about people
situations. F

I'd never feelings things, uck no!

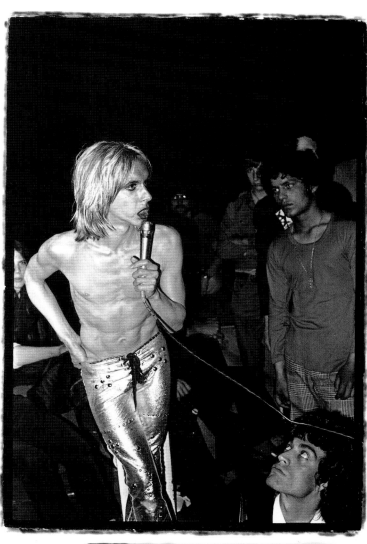

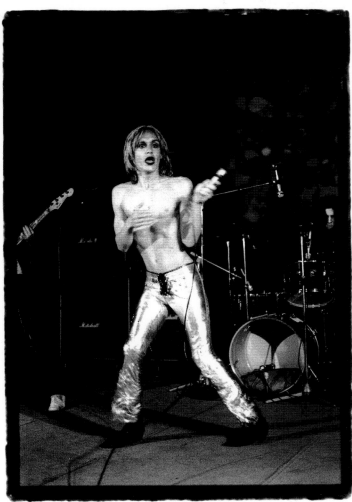

It occurred to me recently (not for the first time) while watching a British TV documentary about him that Ig/Jim was some kind of walking miracle. Not just as a great artist, but also as a human being of indelible character. Somebody up there (or down there) must have gotten their wires totally fucked, for this true original, this key gentleman of the rock 'n' roll realm, should have been nailed in a wooden box or cast to the wind decades ago. But there he was once again, larger than life and at least twice as fabulous, defying all the odds. The great Gods of self-destruction have been salivating over him forever, but the Igman rocks on. His is a wonderful myth of burn-out, rejection and redemption enacted in a classic, almost Greek, mould.

It's been a privilege and a pleasure and I'm glad I've got the pics to bear witness.

May your raw power pump forever, Igmeister.

Thanks for the magic.

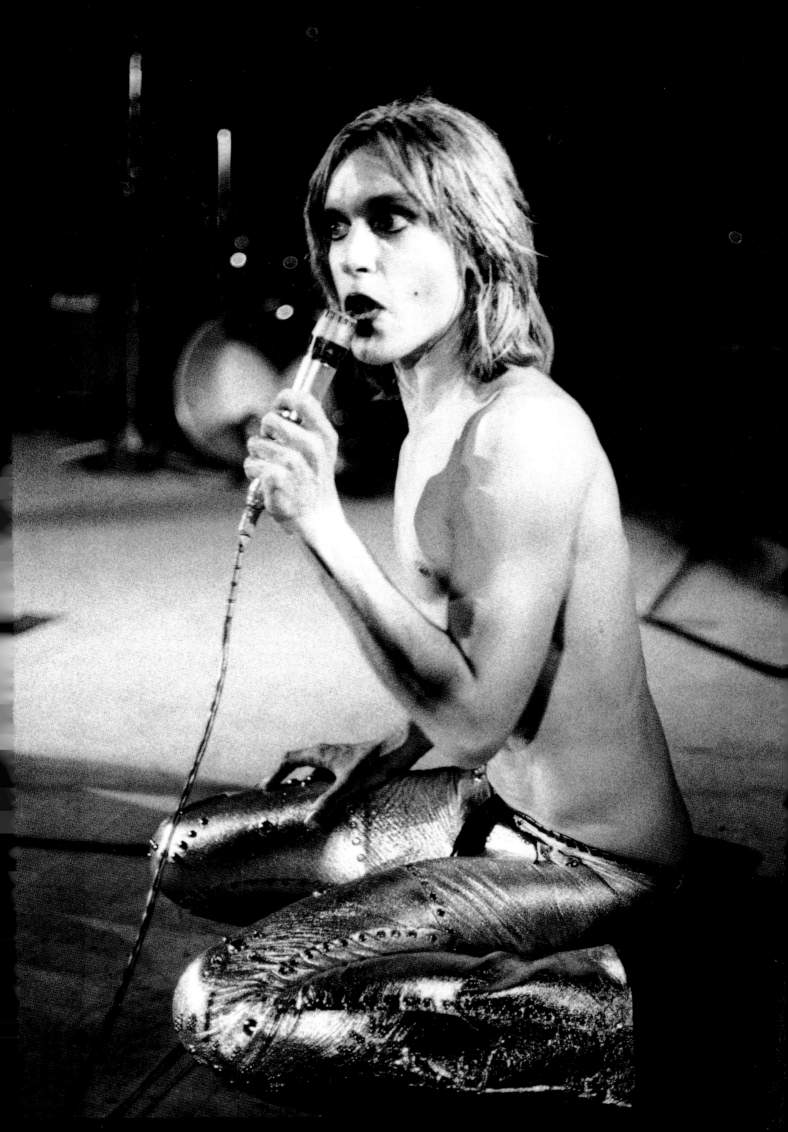

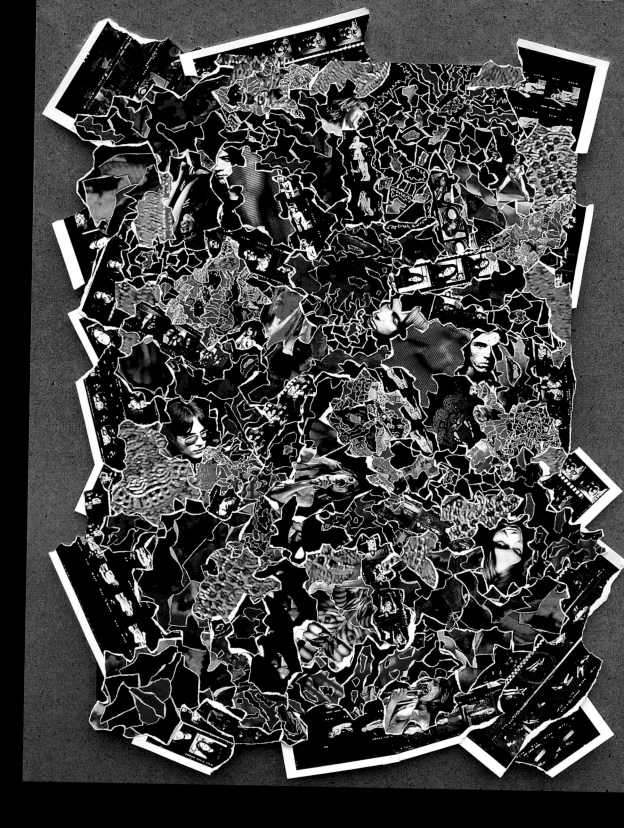

220

TIME AND AGAIN LIFE HAS PROVEN ITSELF TO BE WILD AND UNPREDICTABLE, I'M GRATEFUL TO SAY.

"The Time Is Now And Now Is The Time."

Yogi Bhajan

r Thank Yous to:

sterberg — For his inspired and inspirational alter ego

Asheton, Scott Asheton and James Williamson — For providing the power and the context

Bowie — For his intuitive vision

Charlesworth — For believing in the project

ew Melchior — For wanting it as much as I did and delivering…

Cross — For his superb design

p — For her patience and loyalty

ollins — For his care and support

al thanks to: Pati and Nathalie Rock, Allen Klein, Iris Keitel, Andrew Loog Oldham, Joan Rock,
rd Lasdon, Dean Holtermann, Catherine Alexander, Sat Jivan Kaur, Sat Jivan Singh, Virginia Lohle,
and Lucky of DigiZone, NYC.

Mick Rock Bibliography

**Mick Rock, A Photographic Record 1969-1980** — Century 22 Books 1995
**Blood And Glitter** — VisionOn Books 2001
**Psychedelic Renegades** / Syd Barrett — Genesis Publications 2002
**Moonage Daydream** / Ziggy Stardust (with David Bowie) — Genesis Publications 2002
**Rock'n'Roll Eye** — Tokyo Metropolitan Museum of Photography 2003
**Killer Queen** (with Brian May) — Genesis Publications 2003
**Picture This, Debbie Harry And Blondie** — Sanctuary Publishing 2004

To come: **Transformer** (with Lou Reed) — Genesis Publications 2006

## www.mickrock.com